❧

Presented to:

Julie Ragsdale

By:

The Myers Fam.

Date:

6-5-03

Occasion:

Get Well

This book in its entirety—from literary development to artwork and final design—is a creation of Koechel Peterson & Associates, Inc. Artwork by Katia Andreeva is reproduced under license from Koechel Peterson & Associates, Inc. and may not be reproduced without permission. For information regarding art prints featured in this book, please contact: Koechel Peterson & Associates, Inc., 2600 East 26th Street, Minneapolis, Minnesota 55406; 1-612-721-5017.

Warner Books, Inc., 1271 Avenue of the Americas, New York, NY 10020

Visit our website at www.twbookmark.com

 WARNER *Faith* A Division of AOL Time Warner Book Group
The Warner Faith name and logo are registered trademarks of Warner Books, Inc.

Printed in the United States of America

First Printing: May 2003
10 9 8 7 6 5 4 3 2 1

ISBN: 0-446-53252-5
LCCN: 2003101823

THE POWER OF
BEING POSITIVE

Enjoying God Forever

JOYCE MEYER

WARNER
Faith

CONTENTS

THE POWER OF BEING POSITIVE

Positive minds produce positive lives.
Positive thoughts are always
full of faith and hope.

GOD'S WORD FOR YOU

For as he thinks in his heart, so is he.

PROVERBS 23:7

Then to the centurion Jesus said, Go; it shall be done for you as you have believed. And the servant boy was restored to health at that very moment.

MATTHEW 8:13

one

THE POWER OF BEING POSITIVE

any years ago, I was an extremely negative person. My whole philosophy was this: "If you don't expect anything good to happen, then you won't be disappointed when it doesn't." So many devastating things had happened to me over the years that I was afraid to believe that anything good might happen. Since my thoughts were all negative, so was my mouth; therefore, so was my life.

Perhaps you're like me. You're avoiding hope to protect yourself against being hurt. This type of behavior sets up a negative lifestyle. Everything becomes negative because the thoughts are negative.

When I really began to study the Word and to trust God to restore me, one of the first things I realized was that the negativism had to go. And the longer I serve God, the more I realize the tremendous power in being positive in my thoughts and words.

Our actions are a direct result of our thoughts. A negative mind will result in a negative life. But if we renew our mind according to God's Word, we will, as Romans 12:2 promises, prove in our experience "the good and acceptable and perfect will of God."

It is a vital necessity that we line up our thoughts with God's thoughts. This is a process that will take time and study.

GOD'S WORD FOR YOU

We are assured and know that [God being a partner in their labor] all things work together and are [fitting into a plan] for good to and for those who love God and are called according to [His] design and purpose.

ROMANS 8:28

ALL THINGS WORK FOR GOOD

The apostle Paul does not say that all things are good, but he does say that all things *work together for good*.

Let's say you get in your car, and it won't start. There are two ways you can look at the situation. You can say, "I knew it! It never fails. My plans always flop." Or you can say, "Well, it looks as though I can't leave right now. I'll go later when the car is fixed. In the meantime, I believe this change in plans is going to work out for my good. There is probably some reason I need to be at home today, so I'm going to enjoy my time here."

Paul also tells us in Romans 12:16 to "readily adjust yourself to [people, things]." The idea is that we must learn to become the kind of person who plans things but who doesn't fall apart if that plan doesn't work out.

The choice is ours. Any time we don't get what we want, our feelings will rise up and try to get us into self-pity and a negative attitude. Or we can adjust to the situation and go ahead and enjoy what God has for us no matter what happens.

The pathway to freedom from negativity begins when we face the problem without making excuses for it.

GOD'S WORD FOR YOU

Therefore if any person is [ingrafted] in Christ (the Messiah) he is a new creation (a new creature altogether); the old [previous moral and spiritual condition] has passed away. Behold, the fresh and new has come!

2 CORINTHIANS 5:17

$\mathscr{A}$ New Day

As "a new creation," you don't have to allow the old things that happened to you to keep affecting your new life in Christ. You are a new creature with a new life in Christ. You can have your mind renewed according to the Word of God. Good things are going to happen to you!

Begin to think positively about your life. That doesn't mean that you can get anything you want by just thinking about it. God has a perfect plan for each of us, and we can't control Him with our thoughts and words. But, we must think and speak in agreement with His will and plan for us.

If you don't have any idea what God's will is for you at this point, at least begin by thinking, *Well, I don't know God's plan, but I know He loves me. Whatever He does will be good, and I'll be blessed.*

The hardest part is saying to yourself, "I want to change. I can't change myself, but I believe God will change me as I trust Him. I know it will take time, and I'm not going to get discouraged with myself. *God has begun a good work in me, and He is well able to bring it to full completion*" (see Philippians 1:6).

Jesus will set you free to enjoy the good things in life.
Trust God to renew your mind with His Word!

GOD'S WORD FOR YOU

However, I am telling you nothing but the truth when I say it is profitable (good, expedient, advantageous) for you that I go away. Because if I do not go away, the Comforter (Counselor, Helper, Advocate, Intercessor, Strengthener, Standby) will not come to you [into close fellowship with you]; but if I go away, I will send Him to you [to be in close fellowship with you].

And when He comes, He will convict and convince the world and bring demonstration to it about sin and about righteousness (uprightness of heart and right standing with God) and about judgment.

JOHN 16:7–8

TRUST THE HOLY SPIRIT

Even though I was extremely negative, and although I struggled to keep my mind in a positive pattern, God showed me that if I would trust Him, He would cause me to be very positive. Now, I can't stand negativism. It's similar to the experience of a person who quits smoking and then has no tolerance for cigarettes. I've seen so many good changes in my life since I've been delivered from a negative mind that now I'm opposed to anything negative.

Here's what you need to do. Ask the Holy Spirit to convict you each time you start to get negative. This is part of His work. John 16:7–8 teaches us that the Holy Spirit will convict us of sin and convince us of righteousness. When the conviction comes, ask God to help you. Don't think you can handle this yourself. Lean on Him.

Face reality. If you are sick, don't say, "I'm not sick," because that's just not true. But you can say, "I believe God is healing me." You don't have to say, "I'll probably get worse and end up in the hospital." You can say, "God's healing power is working right now. I believe I'll be all right."

Bring your life into a healthy balance. Ask God to help you have a "ready mind" to deal with whatever happens to you, whether it is positive or negative.

GOD'S WORD FOR YOU

These were more noble than those in Thessalonica, in that they received the word with all readiness of mind, and searched the scriptures daily, whether those things were so.

ACTS 17:11 KJV

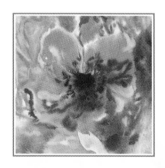

A READY MIND

The Bible says that we are to have a ready mind. That means we are to have minds that are open to the will of God for us, whatever that will may be.

Recently a young lady whom I know experienced the sorrow of a broken engagement. She wanted the relationship to continue and was thinking, hoping, and believing that her former fiancé would feel the same way.

I advised her to have a "ready mind" in case it didn't work out that way. She asked, "Well, isn't that being negative?"

No, it isn't! Negativism would say, "My life is over. No one will ever want me. I'll be miserable forever."

Having a positive mind says, "I'm really sad this happened, but I'm going to trust God. I'm going to ask and believe for our relationship to be restored; but more than anything, I want God's perfect will. If it doesn't turn out the way I want, I'll survive, because Jesus lives in me. It may be hard, but I trust the Lord. I believe that in the end everything will work out for the best."

Practice being positive in every situation that arises.
God has promised to bring good out of whatever
is taking place in your life at the moment.

GOD'S WORD FOR YOU

[For Abraham, human reason for] hope being gone, hoped in faith that he should become the father of many nations, as he had been promised, So [numberless] shall your descendants be.

He did not weaken in faith when he considered the [utter] impotence of his own body, which was as good as dead because he was about a hundred years old, or [when he considered] the barrenness of Sarah's [deadened] womb.

No unbelief or distrust made him waver (doubtingly question) concerning the promise of God, but he grew strong and was empowered by faith as he gave praise and glory to God.

ROMANS 4:18–20

THE FORCE OF HOPE

In our ministry we want to help more people every year, and we believe God wants us to grow. But we also realize that if God has a different plan, and if we end our year with no growth, we cannot let that situation control our joy.

We believe *for* many things, but beyond them all, we believe *in* Someone. That Someone is Jesus. We don't always know what is going to happen. We just know it will always work out for our good!

It is reported that Abraham, after sizing up his situation (he didn't ignore the facts), considered the utter impotence of his own body and the barrenness of Sarah's womb. Although all human reason for hope was gone, he hoped in faith.

Abraham was very positive about a very negative situation!

Hebrews 6:19 tells us that hope is the anchor of the soul. Hope is the force that keeps us steady in a time of trial. Don't ever stop hoping. If you do, you're going to have a miserable life. Don't be afraid to hope. No one can promise that you'll never be disappointed. But you can always have hope and be positive. Put yourself in God's miracle-working realm.

Expect a miracle in your life!

GOD'S WORD FOR YOU

And therefore the Lord [earnestly] waits [expecting, looking, and longing] to be gracious to you; and therefore He lifts Himself up, that He may have mercy on you and show loving-kindness to you. For the Lord is a God of justice. Blessed (happy, fortunate, to be envied) are all those who [earnestly] wait for Him, who expect and look and long for Him [for His victory, His favor, His love, His peace, His joy, and His matchless, unbroken companionship]!

ISAIAH 30:18

⸎

Expect to Receive!

I want to establish firmly in your heart forever that you need to begin to think about what you are thinking about. So many people's problems are rooted in thinking patterns that actually produce the problems they experience in their lives. Remember that your actions are the direct result of your thoughts. And although Satan offers wrong thinking to everyone, you don't need to accept his offer.

Isaiah 30:18 has become one of my favorite Scriptures. If you will meditate on it, it will begin to bring you great hope . . . and great power. In it, God is saying that He is looking for someone to be gracious (good) to, but it cannot be someone with a sour attitude and a negative mind. It must be someone who is expecting (looking and longing) for God to be good to him or her.

Don't ever give up, because little by little you are changing. The more you change your mind for the better, the more your life will also change for the better. When you begin to see God's plan for you in your thinking, you will begin to walk in it.

The mind is the leader or forerunner of all actions.
Always expect good things from God!

GOD'S WORD FOR YOU

All the days of the desponding and afflicted are made evil [by anxious thoughts and forebodings], but he who has a glad heart has a continual feast [regardless of circumstances].

PROVERBS 15:15

Evil Forebodings

An "evil foreboding" is a vague, threatening feeling that something bad is going to happen. There was a point when I realized that I had actually carried these feelings with me most of my life. In fact, I had been made miserable by evil thoughts and forebodings.

Perhaps you have these feelings as well. You have circumstances that are very difficult, but even when you don't, you are still miserable because your thoughts are poisoning your outlook and robbing you of the ability to enjoy life and see good days.

Proverbs 15:15 promises us that these feelings need not remain. Faith's attitude is one of leaning on God, trusting and being confident in Him—it is a joyful feasting on the expectancy of good. Rather than dreading something by anticipating that it will make us miserable, we can have faith that God will give us the power to enjoy it.

Our joy, peace, righteousness, and power are on the *inside* of us through the presence of the Holy Spirit. We need to allow Him to work in power on the *inside* and put less focus on the things *outside* us.

*God's power can fall on us and energize us
to do mundane, everyday tasks with great joy.*

GOD'S WORD FOR YOU

For let him who wants to enjoy life and see good days [good—whether apparent or not] keep his tongue free from evil and his lips from guile (treachery, deceit).

1 PETER 3:10

Death and life are in the power of the tongue, and they who indulge in it shall eat the fruit of it [for death or life].

PROVERBS 18:21

KEEP YOUR TONGUE FROM EVIL

The apostle Peter plainly tells us that enjoying life and seeing good days, and having a positive mind and mouth, are linked together.

Our mouth gives expression to what we think, feel, and want. Our minds tells us what we think, not necessarily what God thinks. Our will tells us what we want, not what God wants. Our emotions tell us what we feel, not what God feels. As our soul is purified, it is trained to carry God's thoughts, desires, and feelings; then we become a mouthpiece for the Lord!

Your words, as reflections of your thoughts, have the power to bring blessing or destruction not only to your life but also to the lives of many others. In 1 Corinthians 2:16, the Word of God teaches us that we have the mind of Christ and that we hold the thoughts, feelings, and purposes of His heart. We hold them in us, but the flesh often blocks them from coming forth. Therein lies the battle—the continual struggle between our flesh and the spirit.

No matter how negative you are or how long you have been that way, I know you can change because I did. It took time and "heaping helpings" of the Holy Spirit, but it was worth it.

THE
BATTLE FOR
THE MIND

*The mind is the battlefield
where our war with Satan
is either won or lost.*

GOD'S WORD FOR YOU

For we are not wrestling with flesh and blood [contending only with physical opponents], but against the despotisms, against the powers, against [the master spirits who are] the world rulers of this present darkness, against the spirit forces of wickedness in the heavenly (supernatural) sphere.

EPHESIANS 6:12

t w o

THE BATTLE FOR THE MIND

A careful study of Ephesians 6 informs us that we are in a war, and that our warfare is not with other human beings but with the devil and his demons. Our enemy, Satan, attempts to defeat us with strategy and deceit, through well-laid plans and deliberate deception.

Jesus called the devil "the father of lies and of all that is false" (John 8:44). He lies to you and me. He tells us things about ourselves, about other people, and about circumstances that are just not true. He does not, however, tell us the entire lie all at one time.

He begins by bombarding our mind with a cleverly devised pattern of little nagging thoughts, suspicions, doubts, fears, wonderings, reasonings, and theories. He moves slowly and cautiously. Remember, he has a strategy for his warfare. He has studied us for a long time.

Satan knows what we like and what we don't like. He knows our insecurities, weaknesses, and fears. He knows what bothers us most and is willing to invest any amount of time it takes to defeat us. His strong point is patience.

*God intends to work through us to defeat the enemy.
He will do it through us!*

GOD'S WORD FOR YOU

*For the weapons of our warfare are not physical
[weapons of flesh and blood], but they are mighty before
God for the overthrow and destruction of strongholds,*

*[Inasmuch as we] refute arguments and theories and
reasonings and every proud and lofty thing that sets itself
up against the [true] knowledge of God; and we lead every
thought and purpose away captive into the obedience of
Christ (the Messiah, the Anointed One) . . .*

2 CORINTHIANS 10:4–5

TEARING DOWN STRONGHOLDS

Through careful strategy and cunning deceit, Satan attempts to set up "strongholds" in our mind. A stronghold is an area in which we are held in bondage (in prison) due to a certain way of thinking. Strongholds are lies that are believed.

The apostle Paul tells us that we have the spiritual weapons we need to overcome Satan's strongholds. Using our weapons, we refute the enemy's lies, arguments, theories, reasonings, and every other thing that tries to exalt itself against the truth of God's Word. We must take our thoughts captive and refuse to indulge in the fleshly luxury of receiving and meditating on every thought that falls into our heads.

The primary weapon with which we do battle is the Word of God used in various ways—preached, taught, sung, confessed, meditated upon, written, and read. We must get the knowledge of God's truth in us to renew our minds. The Word of God has a cleansing effect on our minds and lives any way we use it.

No one will ever live a truly victorious life without being a sincere student of God's Word.

Every stronghold in your mind can be torn down and every deception uncovered. You can win the battle. Don't settle for anything less than complete freedom.

GOD'S WORD FOR YOU

And take the helmet of salvation and the sword that the Spirit wields, which is the Word of God.

EPHESIANS 6:17

If you abide in My word [hold fast to My teachings and live in accordance with them], you are truly My disciples.

And you will know the Truth, and the Truth will set you free.

JOHN 8:31–32

THE SWORD OF THE SPIRIT

The attacks of Satan against the church are more intense than ever before. More people than ever are experiencing tremendous attacks against their minds and enduring great attacks of fear.

A person who learns to abide in the Word of God and let the Word abide in him will have a two-edged sword with which to do battle. To abide means to remain, to continue in, or to dwell in. If you make God's Word a small part of your life, you will know only a partial truth and will experience only limited freedom, but those who *abide* in it will know the full truth and will experience complete freedom.

I can testify that the Word of God has caused me to be victorious over the devil. My life was a mess because I was ignorant of the Word. I had been a Christian for many years who loved God and was active in church work. But I had zero victory because I did not know the Word.

Learn the Word and allow the Holy Spirit to wield it by speaking, singing, or meditating on the portions of Scripture that you feel He is placing on your heart.

If you keep your sword drawn, the enemy won't be so quick to approach you. Speak the Word!

GOD'S WORD FOR YOU

Pray at all times (on every occasion, in every season) in the Spirit, with all [manner of] prayer and entreaty. To that end keep alert and watch with strong purpose and perseverance, interceding in behalf of all the saints (God's consecrated people).

EPHESIANS 6:18

PRAYING IN THE SPIRIT

Prayer is another spiritual weapon God has given us to wage warfare. Prayer is relationship with the Godhead. It is coming and asking for help or talking to God about something that bothers us.

If you want to have an effective prayer life, develop a good personal relationship with the Father. Know that He loves you, that He is full of mercy, that He will help you. Get to know Jesus. He is your Friend. He died for you. Get to know the Holy Spirit. He is with you all the time as your Helper. Let Him help you.

All kinds of prayer are to be used in our walk with God. There is the prayer of agreement between two people and also the united prayer of a group of people. There are prayers of thanksgiving, praise and worship, petition, intercession, commitment, and consecration.

Whatever kind of prayer you bring, learn to fill your prayers with the Word of God and offer them with the assurance that God keeps His Word. God's Word and our need are the basis on which we come to Him.

The more time a person spends meditating on the Word, the more he will reap from the Word.

GOD'S WORD FOR YOU

Let the saints be joyful in the glory and beauty [which God confers upon them]; let them sing for joy upon their beds.

Let the high praises of God be in their throats and a two-edged sword in their hands.

PSALM 149:5–6

HIGH PRAISES OF GOD

In David's Psalm 149, he gives us a picture of the position that the saints of God should take—with songs of praise and worship in their throats and the two-edged sword of the Word of God in their hands. In the remainder of the psalm, he goes on to infer that this position is taken by the saints in order to defeat their enemies.

Praise defeats the devil quicker than any other battle plan. Praise is a garment that we put on and that will protect us from defeat and negativity in our minds. But it must be genuine heart praise, not just lip service or a method being tried to see if it works. Also, praise involves the Word. We praise God according to His Word and His goodness.

Worship is a battle position! As we worship God for Who He is and for His attributes, for His ability and might, we will see His power and attributes released on our behalf.

I am sure your heart frequently fills up with love and worship for God. Bow your heart and give thanks to Him. Praise and worship confuse the enemy. Take your position, and you will see the enemy's defeat.

God never loses a battle. He has a definite battle plan, and when we follow it, we always win.

GOD'S WORD FOR YOU

For no temptation (no trial regarded as enticing to sin, no matter how it comes or where it leads) has overtaken you and laid hold on you that is not common to man [that is, no temptation or trial has come to you that is beyond human resistance and that is not adjusted and adapted and belonging to human experience, and such as man can bear]. But God is faithful [to His Word and to His compassionate nature], and He [can be trusted] not to let you be tempted and tried and assayed beyond your ability and strength of resistance and power to endure, but with the temptation He will [always] also provide the way out (the means of escape to a landing place), that you may be capable and strong and powerful to bear up under it patiently.

1 CORINTHIANS 10:13

NEVER AN EXCUSE

Sadly, many people do not always accept the truth that God reveals to them. It is painful to face our faults and deal with them. We tend to justify misbehavior. We allow our past and how we were raised to negatively affect the rest of our lives.

Our past may explain why we're suffering, but we must not use it as an excuse to stay in bondage.

Everyone is without excuse because Jesus always stands ready to fulfill His promise to set us free. He will walk us across the finish line in any area if we are willing to go all the way through it with Him.

Thank God, we have the weapons to tear down the strongholds. God doesn't abandon us and leave us helpless. He promises us that He will not allow us to be tempted beyond what we can bear, but with every temptation He will also provide the way out, the escape.

You may have some major strongholds in your life that need to be broken. Let me encourage you by saying, "God is on your side." In the spiritual battle going on in your mind, God is fighting on your side.

❧

No matter how great the temptation before us, God has promised us everything we need to walk in victory.

God's Word for You

Behold! I have given you authority and power to trample upon serpents and scorpions, and [physical and mental strength and ability] over all the power that the enemy [possesses]; and nothing shall in any way harm you.

Luke 10:19

You Have the Power

Far too many believers are fainthearted, weak in determination, and diseased with an "I can't" attitude. They are plagued with a lack of spiritual power.

You and I don't have to beg God to give us power. We just need to realize and accept that we have been given power and then walk in what is already ours. We must develop and maintain a "power consciousness"—an aggressive, power-packed attitude.

God has given us spiritual power for spiritual warfare. Spiritual power is released when our faith is firm. When we walk in faith we can approach every situation with an enemy-conquering attitude.

An attitude of confidence will exude from us when we know who we are in Christ, and believe in the power that the Bible says is ours through faith.

Do you desire to be a powerful believer? Try approaching every situation in your life with a simple, childlike faith—believing that God is good, that He has a good plan for your life, and that He is working in your situation.

You have the power and authority of the name of Jesus.
Walk in the strength of His conquering name!

GOD'S WORD FOR YOU

For those who are according to the flesh and are controlled by its unholy desires set their minds on and pursue those things which gratify the flesh, but those who are according to the Spirit and are controlled by the desires of the Spirit set their minds on and seek those things which gratify the [Holy] Spirit.

ROMANS 8:5

WHO CONTROLS THE MIND?

In the *King James Version*, the eighth chapter of Romans teaches us that if we "mind" the flesh, we will walk in the flesh. But if we "mind" the things of the Spirit, we will walk in the Spirit.

Let me put it another way: If we think fleshly thoughts, wrong thoughts, negative thoughts, we cannot walk in the Spirit. It seems as if renewed, godlike thinking is a vital necessity to a successful Christian life.

Your life may be in a state of chaos because of years of wrong thinking. If so, it is important for you to come to grips with the fact that *your life will not get straightened out until your mind does.* You should consider this area one of *vital necessity.*

You cannot overcome your situation by determination alone. You do need to be determined, but determined in the Holy Spirit, not in the effort of your own flesh. The Holy Spirit is your Helper—seek His help. Lean on Him. You can't make it alone.

Give the Holy Spirit control of your life. He will lead you into the perfect will of God for you, which includes exceeding, abundant blessings, peace, and joy.

GOD'S WORD FOR YOU

Either make the tree sound (healthy and good), and its fruit sound (healthy and good), or make the tree rotten (diseased and bad), and its fruit rotten (diseased and bad); for the tree is known and recognized and judged by its fruit.

MATTHEW 12:33

A VITAL NECESSITY

For the believer, right thinking is something that is so important that one simply cannot live without it—like a heartbeat is vital, or blood pressure is vital. There are things without which there is no life. Our life source, our source for right thinking, is regular, personal fellowship with God in prayer and the Word.

The Bible says that a tree is known by its fruit.

The same is true of our lives. Thoughts bear fruit. Think good thoughts, and the fruit of your life will be good. Think bad thoughts, and the fruit in your life will be bad.

Actually, you can look at a person's attitude and know what kind of thinking is prevalent in his life. A sweet, kind person does not have mean, vindictive thoughts. By the same token, a truly evil person does not have good, loving thoughts.

Remember Proverbs 23:7 and allow it to have an impact on your life: for as you think in your heart, so are you.

When we wait in God's presence, there is a divine exchange. We exchange our nothingness for His everything. Our weakness is swallowed up in His strength.

A Heart
That
Hinders

*While the world is busy trying
to conquer "outer space," we should
strive to conquer "inner space."*

GOD'S WORD FOR YOU

Keep thy heart with all diligence; for out of it are the issues of life.

PROVERBS 4:23 KJV

Amaziah was twenty-five years old when he began to reign, and he reigned twenty-nine years in Jerusalem. . . .

He did right in the Lord's sight, but not with a perfect or blameless heart.

2 CHRONICLES 25:1–2

three

A HEART THAT HINDERS

hen God speaks to us about our heart, He is asking for our entire life, the entire personality, character, body, mind, and emotions in the spirit of a person. The heart is the real person, not the person everybody sees.

The heart is the most important aspect of the spiritual body, and the heart attitude should be the major issue of every believer. It is not lack of ability or potential that prevents most people from making progress and enjoying fulfillment in life. It is wrong heart attitudes that negatively affect our minds and thoughts.

There are many conditions of the heart. Some are positive, and some are negative. King Amaziah is noted for having a negative condition of the heart. He did all the right things, but his heart was not right. Therefore, God was not pleased with him. That's a scary thing. We can do the right thing, and yet have it not be acceptable to God because we do it with a wrong heart attitude.

God is more concerned about your heart than He is about what you do, because if your heart is right, what you do will eventually catch up with that. Who you are in your heart is reflected in your thoughts and attitudes.

GOD'S WORD FOR YOU

The Lord saw that the wickedness of man was great in the earth, and that every imagination and intention of all human thinking was only evil continually.

And the Lord regretted that He had made man on the earth, and He was grieved at heart.

So the Lord said, I will destroy, blot out, and wipe away mankind, whom I have created from the face of the ground. . . .

But Noah found grace (favor) in the eyes of the Lord.

GENESIS 6:5–8

An Evil Heart

The story of Noah tells us that many people today are being destroyed for the simple reason that their hearts are wrong. There were three heart issues concerning the people of Noah's day that displeased God: wickedness, evil imaginations, and evil thinking. But Noah had a right heart and found favor in the eyes of the Lord.

We cannot imagine how many areas of our lives would get straightened out if we would just get our hearts right with God. Our hearts may not be filled with the exact same evil thoughts and imaginations of the people in Noah's day, but a bad attitude or wrong thinking can also be labeled evil imaginations and evil thinking. If we have a bad attitude and "stinking thinking," we are going nowhere in life.

This is why we must guard our heart—because out of it flow the issues of our life. Our problem is that if we let garbage in, garbage will come back out. Allowing negative, evil thinking in our hearts cannot produce a life that glorifies God. We have to be careful not only about our actions but also about our imagination, our intent, our motivation, our attitude. If we fail here, we may end up with an evil heart.

We need a tender heart that deals immediately with a bad attitude about anything or anyone.

GOD'S WORD FOR YOU

Therefore, as the Holy Spirit says: Today, if you will hear His voice,

Do not harden your hearts, as [happened] in the rebellion [of Israel] and their provocation and embitterment [of Me] in the day of testing in the wilderness.

HEBREWS 3:7–8

[Therefore beware] brethren, take care, lest there be in any one of you a wicked, unbelieving heart [which refuses to cleave to, trust in, and rely on Him], leading you to turn away and desert or stand aloof from the living God.

HEBREWS 3:12

A Hard, Unbelieving Heart

In Hebrews 3 we see two wrong conditions of the heart—a hard heart and an unbelieving heart. In the wilderness, a hard heart caused the Israelites to rebel. A person with a hard heart cannot believe God easily, which is a major problem because everything we receive from God comes through believing. To receive from Him, we must come to Him in simple, childlike faith and just believe.

We call ourselves believers, but the truth is, there are a lot of "unbelieving believers." For a long time, I was one of them. I had been hurt so much during my childhood, I developed a hardness of heart that God had to break through in my life.

Even Moses got to the place in the wilderness where he was slow of heart to believe God. That's why we have to stay sharp spiritually if we are going to be quick to believe and to walk in faith day by day. We must be careful to go from faith to faith and not begin to mix in any doubt and unbelief.

Remember that Jesus wants to restore your soul, including your emotions. Let Jesus into those areas of your life that no one else could ever reach. Ask Him to change you into a person after His heart, a person who has the same kind of heart that He has.

GOD'S WORD FOR YOU

. . . he who has a haughty look and a proud and arrogant heart I cannot and I will not tolerate.

PSALM 101:5

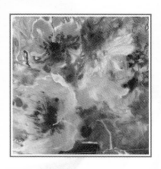

A PROUD HEART

Has God ever had to deal with you about pride? From personal experience I can tell you that a proud person hates to admit his problem with pride.

How can you tell if you have a problem with pride? If you have an opinion about everything, if you are judgmental, if you can't be corrected, if you rebel against authority, if you want to take all the credit for yourself, or if you say "I" too often, you have a problem with pride.

It is hard to let God get all that pride stuff out of us, but it is vital. If we want to experience the power of being positive, we must realize it flows out of an attitude of humility. When we recognize we are not always right about everything, it makes us teachable and willing to take correction. It is only in the place of humility that God can bless us.

The enemy will attack and tempt you with a spirit of pride. It takes effort to keep a right heart. One of the most powerful things we have to guard against is a spirit of self-righteousness.

We have it backward if we think that everything in our life would be fine if the devil just left us alone. If we live right, the devil has no power over us.

GOD'S WORD FOR YOU

Therefore you have no excuse or defense or justification, O man, whoever you are who judges and condemns another. For in posing as judge and passing sentence on another, you condemn yourself, because you who judge are habitually practicing the very same things [that you censure and denounce].

ROMANS 2:1

A HYPOCRITICAL HEART

Anyone who judges and condemns other people for doing the same things he does has to be deceived. Yet to some degree, we all do that. We tend to look at ourselves through rose-colored glasses while looking at everyone else through a magnifying glass. We excuse our wrong behavior, while claiming that others who do the same things we do are deserving of judgment.

That kind of attitude is hypocritical and the same as the scribes and Pharisees of Jesus' day. Jesus noted that they put on a big show of being holy while refusing to help anybody (Matthew 23:2–4). Proud and haughty, they did good works only to be seen by the crowds and to be thought of as great and important.

All of that kind of fleshly glory means nothing to God. He is looking for people with a right heart so He can bless us. Our degree of spiritual maturity is not measured by how much we read the Bible or accomplish, but by how much we promptly obey God's Word and by how we treat other people.

If there is pride in our lives, God is obligated to show us our flaws. He does not do it to embarrass us or to make us feel bad about ourselves, but to keep us in a place where we are dependent upon Him and merciful with other people who have faults.

GOD'S WORD FOR YOU

The heart knows its own bitterness, and no stranger shares its joy.

PROVERBS 14:10

For if you forgive people their trespasses [their reckless and willful sins, leaving them, letting them go, and giving up resentment], your heavenly Father will also forgive you.

MATTHEW 6:14

A Bitter, Unforgiving Heart

One of the most dangerous heart conditions we can have is unforgiveness. If we do not forgive others, we will not be forgiven, and our faith will not work. And everything that comes from God comes by faith. If our faith doesn't work, we are in serious trouble.

"But you don't know what was done to me," people always say to try to excuse their bitterness, resentment, and unforgiveness. Based on what the Bible says, it really doesn't matter how great their offense was. We serve a God Who is greater, and if we will handle the offense in the right way, He will bring justice and recompense.

Jesus taught us that we are to forgive those who hurt us, pray for those who despitefully use us, and bless those who curse us. That is hard. But there is something harder—being full of hatred, bitterness, and resentment. Don't spend your life hating someone who is probably out having a good time while you are all upset.

Never try to get people back for what they have done to you. Forgive them and leave them in God's hands.

Power in the Christian life comes from love, not from hatred, bitterness, and unforgiveness.

GOD'S WORD FOR YOU

When you go forth to battle against your enemies and see horses and chariots and an army greater than your own, do not be afraid of them, for the Lord your God, Who brought you out of the land of Egypt, is with you.

And when you come near to the battle, the priest shall approach and speak to the men,

And shall say to them, Hear, O Israel, you draw near this day to battle against your enemies. Let not your [minds and] hearts faint; fear not, and do not tremble or be terrified [and in dread] because of them.

For the Lord your God is He Who goes with you to fight for you against your enemies to save you.

DEUTERONOMY 20:1–4

A FAINT HEART

Fainthearted people are people who give up easily. When the heart faints, it just gives up. It has to have everything a certain way or it quits. It gets discouraged and depressed quickly. The person gets his feelings hurt easily. Everything bothers him. He is touchy. In his heart he says, "I can't do this. It's just too hard."

In Proverbs 24:10 we are told, *If you faint in the day of adversity, your strength is small.* We can never stand against the enemy if we are fainthearted. And if we would enjoy the power of a positive mind, we cannot be wimpy or a quitter.

All of us have to resist against getting tired and giving up because we are being hassled by the devil. With God's strength, we don't have to faint, no matter what kind of adversity we are facing. The best way to fight the devil, especially in times of challenge and stress, is to just stay calm, to maintain a peaceful, gentle heart. Be constant, be fearless. That is a sign to the devil of his impending destruction.

And we must not be fainthearted with God's correction of our lives. When God is dealing with us, sometimes He has to do it over and over. Molding is never fun, but we will reap if we do not faint.

God's power is available to break a fainthearted spirit.

GOD'S WORD FOR YOU

Trust in the LORD *with all your heart,*
And lean not on your own understanding;
In all your ways acknowledge Him,
And He shall direct your paths.

PROVERBS 3:5–6 NKJV

A REASONING HEART

People who must reason out everything have a very hard time with faith because reasoning is not faith, and without faith it is impossible to please God.

I used to be a class A, chief reasoner. I had to have everything figured out. I had to have a plan if I was going to be positive. I was continually asking, "Why, God, why? When, God, when?" Then one day the Lord spoke to my heart and said, "As long as you continue to reason, you will never have discernment."

Discernment starts in the heart and moves up and enlightens the mind. As long as my mind was so busy reasoning apart from the Holy Spirit and contrary to the truth in the Word of God, Jesus could not get through to me. He wants us to use our mind to reason, but He wants us to reason in a way that lines up with His Word.

Balance is the key to victory in our minds. It is fine and necessary to make plans, but you cannot allow yourself to be controlled and manipulated by those plans. Say to the Lord, "You know the way, and I will be satisfied with that. When You are ready to show me, do so. Until then, I'll enjoy it and trust You."

If we try to figure out why everything happens in life,
we will not have peace of mind and heart.

GOD'S WORD FOR YOU

For ye are yet carnal: for whereas there is among you envying, and strife, and divisions, are ye not carnal, and walk as men?

1 CORINTHIANS 3:3 KJV

An Envious Heart

Envy and jealousy cause us to strive after things that God will give us in His timing, if it is His will that we have them. A jealous, envious heart in no way blesses God, and the negativity spills out over others that He means to bless through our lives.

We need to be happy with what God has given us. We need to trust Him that if we are supposed to have more, He will give it to us when He knows we are able to handle it.

But you may feel that the devil is keeping you from being blessed. Look at it this way. If you are doing what God wants you to do, and your heart is right before Him, no man on earth or devil in hell can keep you from having what God wants you to have.

Many times, blaming everything on the devil is just an excuse not to grow up. It is an excuse not to develop personal character and let God do the work on the inside of us that He wants to do. Instead of focusing on the works of the enemy, we need to keep our eyes on God and let Him have His way in our lives.

God has a tailor-made, personalized plan for our lives. The key to happiness and fulfillment is trusting God to perform His good plan in our lives until we see results.

THE POWER
OF A RENEWED
HEART

*It is not the show we put on for others
on the outside that matters; it is the truth
inside us that we cannot hide from God.*

GOD'S WORD FOR YOU

*For the Lord sees not as man sees; for man looks on
the outward appearance, but the Lord looks on the heart.*

1 SAMUEL 16:7

four
THE POWER OF A RENEWED HEART

od is the God of hearts. He does not look only at the exterior of a person, or even the things a person does, and judge the individual by that criterion. Man judges after the flesh, but God judges by the heart.

It is possible to do good works and still have a wrong heart attitude. It is also possible to do some things wrong but still have a right heart on the inside. God is much more inclined to use a person with a good heart and a few problems than He is to use a person who seems to have it all together but who has a wicked heart.

It is very important that we get in touch with our inner life and our heart attitude, the way we feel and think about things, what the Bible calls the hidden man of the heart, if we want to have any success as a Christian.

When God seeks to promote,
He chooses a person after His own heart.

GOD'S WORD FOR YOU

And the Lord said to Moses,
Speak to the Israelites, that they take for Me an
offering. From every man who gives it willingly and
ungrudgingly with his heart you shall take My offering.

EXODUS 25:1–2

Let each one [give] as he has made up his own mind
and purposed in his heart, not reluctantly or sorrowfully
or under compulsion, for God loves (He takes pleasure in,
prizes above other things, and is unwilling to abandon or
to do without) a cheerful (joyous, "prompt to do it") giver
[whose heart is in his giving].

2 CORINTHIANS 9:7

A WILLING HEART

When we talk about a willing heart, we are basically talking about "want to." If there is something we want to do strongly enough, somehow we will find a way to do it. With it we can lose weight, keep our house clean, save money, get out of debt, or reach any other goal in life we may have set for ourselves. Our victory or defeat has a lot to do with our "want to."

We are really good at laying the blame for our failures on the devil, other people, the past, and on and on. But the truth is that most of the time the bottom line is we just don't have enough of the right kind of "want to."

God examines our heart attitude, and whatever we do for Him must be done willingly. God delights in those who give to Him willingly, joyfully, and cheerfully, but not those who give legalistically or under compulsion. I don't believe we receive any reward for doing things with a bad attitude.

We don't always feel like doing what we want to do, but it is not necessary that we feel like doing it, only that we want to do it.

GOD'S WORD FOR YOU

That is why I would remind you to stir up (rekindle the embers of, fan the flame of, and keep burning) the [gracious] gift of God, [the inner fire] that is in you by means of the laying on of my hands [with those of the elders at your ordination].

2 TIMOTHY 1:6

A STIRRED HEART

God wants us to stay stirred up. It doesn't do any good to say, "I wish I felt that way." You have to decide to do something about the way you feel. If you want to have victory over your feelings strongly enough, you will do whatever it takes to get it.

How do we stay on fire? I have discovered that the Word of God coming out of my own mouth in the form of prayer, praise, preaching, or confessions is the best way that I can find to fan the fire. It stirs up the gift within, keeps the fire aflame, and prevents my spirit from sinking within me.

Passivity, procrastination, and laziness are the tools that Satan uses against God's people. A passive person waits to be moved by an outside force before taking action. We are to be motivated and led by the Holy Spirit within us, not by outside forces. The best way to guard against passivity is to do it with all your might.

Keep your God-given gift,
that fire within you, stirred up.

GOD'S WORD FOR YOU

And thou shalt speak unto all that are wise hearted,
whom I have filled with the spirit of wisdom.

EXODUS 28:3 KJV

A WISE HEART

I am absolutely amazed by some of the stupid things we do. We wonder why we don't have the things in life we want, when all we have to do is watch how we act.

In the book of Haggai we see a group of people who did not like their circumstances at all. God's response to them was, "consider your ways and set your mind on what has come to you" (1:5). For eighteen years they had put off something God had shown them to do, and yet they could not understand why they were not prospering.

We must use wisdom in anything we do in life. It shows up in the way we talk, act, handle our money, meet our responsibilities, treat other people, keep our word, and in a thousand other ways. There are all kinds of ways we have to walk in wisdom, yet so many of God's people are totally stressed out because they are going in ninety-five different directions at once.

Without wisdom, we will never experience the power of being positive.

One of the greatest tragedies in this life is that so many of God's people are just not operating in wisdom.

GOD'S WORD FOR YOU

For the eyes of the LORD run to and fro throughout the whole earth, to shew himself strong in the behalf of them whose heart is perfect toward him.

2 CHRONICLES 16:9 KJV

A PERFECT HEART

What does it mean to have a perfect heart? It means to have a heartfelt desire to do right and to please God. A person who has a perfect heart truly loves God, though he himself may not be perfect. He may still have things in the flesh to deal with. His mouth may still get him into trouble. He may make mistakes or lose his temper. But when he does, he is quick to repent and make it right with God again. If he has offended someone else, he will humble himself and apologize.

When God looks into our lives, He doesn't look for somebody with a perfect performance but a terrible heart attitude. He looks for someone who may not have a perfect performance but who has a right attitude toward Him. If we have a perfect heart toward God, He counts us as perfect and works with us while we are trying to manifest that perfection.

*Having a blameless heart will make a
major difference in your life.*

GOD'S WORD FOR YOU

*And become useful and helpful and kind to one
another, tenderhearted (compassionate, understanding,
loving-hearted), forgiving one another [readily and freely],
as God in Christ forgave you.*

EPHESIANS 4:32

*But the [Holy] Spirit distinctly and expressly declares
that in latter times some will turn away from the faith,
giving attention to deluding and seducing spirits and
doctrines that demons teach,*

*Through the hypocrisy and pretensions of liars whose
consciences are seared (cauterized) . . .*

1 TIMOTHY 4:1–2

A Tender Heart

Having a tender heart is equivalent to having a tender conscience, and tenderness of conscience is vital in our relationship with God. It is dangerous to become hard-hearted and to develop a seared conscience so that we can't really tell if we are doing anything wrong or not. The key is to learn to quickly repent whenever God convicts us of something, not make excuses.

When God shows you that you have done something wrong, just say, "You're right, Lord, I'm wrong. I have no excuse, so please forgive me and help me not to do it again."

It is amazing how much that will help us have a tender conscience toward God and a positive mind. But as soon as we try to reason things out and make excuses for our wrongs, we start getting a little callous on our conscience. It becomes just a little bit harder for us to feel than the time before.

If we have a willing, stirred-up, wise, perfect, and tender heart, the devil may as well get out of our way because nothing can stop us from being positive for God.

GOD'S WORD FOR YOU

My heart is fixed, O God, my heart is steadfast and confident! I will sing and make melody.

PSALM 57:7

A STEADFAST HEART

To have a fixed heart means to have our mind made up so that we are not going to change it. If we are going to experience any kind of victory and be positive in our lives, we must be determined. If we are going to see the fulfillment of God's will, walk in or follow the leading of the Spirit, or accomplish anything worthwhile in this life, we must set our face like flint.

And we must understand that the devil is not going to roll out a red carpet for us just because we decide to get saved and serve God. He is going to oppose us at every turn.

The problem is that because of the mentality of our society, we are always looking for something easy. We've got to be determined to do the will of God, to stay positive and happy, and to walk in the peace of God. His will won't just happen in our life. We are partners with God, and we must do our part. Part of what we have to do is never give up!

Press on with "holy determination,"
and God's plan will be fulfilled in your life.

GOD'S WORD FOR YOU

Though a host encamp against me, my heart shall not fear; though war arise against me, [even then] in this will I be confident.

PSALM 27:3

A CONFIDENT HEART

Not only must our heart be fixed and steadfast, it must also be confident. I have discovered that staying confident is a key to being positive in my mind and overall life.

The devil is constantly trying to introduce thoughts into my head to make me lose my confidence. The mind is the battlefield, and the devil lies to everyone through wrong thinking. The one thing that he's trying to steal all the time is our confidence.

The devil doesn't want us to have confidence in prayer. He doesn't want us to believe we can hear from God. He discourages us concerning the call of God on our life. He wants us to go around feeling like a failure.

We need to confidently declare what the Word says about us, such as, "I am more than a conqueror through Jesus. I can do all things through Christ Who strengthens me. I am triumphant in every situation because God always causes me to triumph." We need to read the Word to the devil, saying, "Is that what you think? Well, just listen to this!"

*We need to get up every morning
prepared to keep Satan under our feet.*

GOD'S WORD FOR YOU

A merry heart does good, like medicine, but a broken spirit dries the bones.

PROVERBS 17:22 NKJV

The thief comes only in order to steal and kill and destroy. I came that they may have and enjoy life, and have it in abundance (to the full, till it overflows).

JOHN 10:10

A MERRY HEART

God is life, and every good thing He created is part of that life. We get so caught up in doing and accomplishing, in working and keeping our commitments, that if we are not careful, we will come to the end of our life and suddenly wake up and realize that we never really lived. God wants us to enjoy life and live it to the full, till it overflows.

We have a choice in life. We can grumble our way through our troubles, or we can sing our way through our troubles with a merry heart. Either way, we have to go through troubles, so why not take the joy of the Lord as our strength and be filled with energy and vitality.

In John 15 Jesus talks about abiding in Him. In verse 11 He says, "I have told you these things, that My joy and delight may be in you, and that your joy and gladness may be of full measure and complete and overflowing." Jesus wants us to have a merry heart. He wants us to put a smile on our face so everybody around us can feel happy and secure.

Don't spend your life waiting for things to change before you can become happy. Learn to be happy now.

The Power
of a Positive
Heart

❦

*God has given us a tool to keep ourselves
radically happy and peaceful.
All we have to do is believe.*

GOD'S WORD FOR YOU

But without faith it is impossible to please and be satisfactory to Him. For whoever would come near to God must [necessarily] believe that God exists and that He is the rewarder of those who earnestly and diligently seek Him [out].

HEBREWS 11:6

five

THE POWER OF A POSITIVE HEART

A positive, believing heart is one of the heart attitudes that is absolutely vital in our relationship with God. That may sound funny, since we are called believers. Don't we all have a believing heart? No, we don't. The church is full of "unbelieving believers."

In Matthew 8:13, Jesus says that it shall be done for you as you have believed. It is amazing how much we can do if we believe we can do it. We need to get up and start every day by saying over and over, "I believe I can; I believe I can."

When the devil starts screaming in our ears that we can't get what we are believing God for, we need the heart and mind of Joshua and Caleb that says, "Let's go and take the Promised Land because we are well able to do so." We need to have the kind of believing heart that says, "What do You want me to do, Lord? Whatever it is, I'll do it!"

To live as God intends us to live, the first thing we need to do is truly believe that it is God's will for us to experience continual joy. Joy and peace are found in believing, and nowhere else.

GOD'S WORD FOR YOU

And I will give them one heart [a new heart] and I will put a new spirit within them; and I will take the stony [unnaturally hardened] heart out of their flesh, and will give them a heart of flesh [sensitive and responsive to the touch of their God].

EZEKIEL 11:19

A NEW HEART

The Bible says that we have to have a new heart. In Ezekiel 11 God promises to give His people a new heart to replace the stony, hardened heart that is in them. This new heart will be sensitive and responsive to Him.

This promise is repeated in Ezekiel 36:26 in which the Lord says, "A new heart will I give you and a new spirit will I put within you, and I will take away the stony heart out of your flesh and give you a heart of flesh."

Through the New Birth, or spiritual birth, we receive Jesus in our heart. It takes us out of the worldly way of living and places us "into Christ" and a new way of thinking, speaking, and acting. But even after that experience, we are told that we must have our minds completely renewed (Romans 12:1). In Ephesians 4:23 we read that we are to be constantly renewed in the spirit of our mind, having a fresh mental and spiritual attitude. Attitudes begin in the mind. Our mind is renewed by the Word of God.

We need an attitude adjustment every day,
and often many times during the day,
because it is so easy to develop a wrong attitude.

GOD'S WORD FOR YOU

My son, *if you will receive my words and treasure up my commandments within you,*

Making your ear attentive to skillful and godly Wisdom and inclining and directing your heart and mind to understanding [applying all your powers to the quest for it];

Yes, if you cry out for insight and raise your voice for understanding,

If you seek [Wisdom] as for silver and search for skillful and godly Wisdom as for hidden treasures,

Then you will understand the reverent and worshipful fear of the Lord and find the knowledge of [our omniscient] God.

PROVERBS 2:1–5

An Understanding Heart

I honestly believe that in the church today we are too selfish and self-centered. All of our thoughts are about ourselves. If we would think—really think— about others, we would be more inclined to do more positive things for them.

We need to seek understanding—to understand God's Word and will, to understand ourselves, and to understand other people. One reason we don't understand other people is that they are not like us. We think that if others are different from us, there must be something wrong with them.

An understanding heart is one of the positive heart conditions we must have. One way we understand what people are going through is by going through it ourselves. It is amazing how caring and compassionate we are when we have gone through a few problems of our own, and how flippant and judgmental we can be if we have not had the same problem ourselves.

We gain an understanding heart by seeking God.

GOD'S WORD FOR YOU

This is the [Lord's] purpose that is purposed upon the whole earth [regarded as conquered and put under tribute by Assyria]; and this is [His omnipotent] hand that is stretched out over all the nations.

For the Lord of hosts has purposed, and who can annul it? And His hand is stretched out, and who can turn it back?

ISAIAH 14:26–27

A PURPOSED HEART

God is a God of purpose, and when He purposes something, it is going to come to pass. Jesus knew His purpose. He said that He came into the world that we might have life and that He might destroy the works of the devil (John 10:10; 1 John 3:8).

Too many Christians don't know their purpose and feel useless and worthless. God wants all of us to enjoy ourselves and to enjoy the life He has given us. But as far as our specific purpose, that varies from person to person and from one season of life to the next.

Whatever we do, we should do it purposefully. We don't love because we feel like it; we do it because we purpose to love others. So with giving, or being merciful, being kind, or walking in the Spirit. Love, joy, peace, patience, kindness, goodness, and all the other fruit of the Spirit are ours to enjoy and to release to others if we do it on purpose. We do these things, not because we always necessarily feel like it, but because it is what we are called to do.

If we want to be positive with our life, we must purpose to be positive because the devil will try to stop us a hundred times a day.

GOD'S WORD FOR YOU

But Mary was keeping within herself all these things
(sayings), weighing and pondering them in her heart.

LUKE 2:19

A PONDERING HEART

God does not want us to have a reasoning heart. He doesn't want us trying to figure out everything in life. But He does want us to ponder.

We can tell when we have moved from pondering to reasoning by the confusion we experience. If we are confused, then we are not pondering in our heart; we are reasoning in our mind.

Mary had some pretty serious things happen in her life. She was just a sweet, little girl who loved God when an angel of the Lord appeared to her and told her she was going to become the mother of the Son of God. But whatever Mary may have thought or felt, she controlled it because she said to the angel, "Let it be unto me according to the Word of God."

When God speaks something to us, many times we need to keep it to ourselves. If He tells us things we don't really understand, things that seem to make no sense, we need to do a little more pondering instead of running to others for advice. We need to zip our lip and ask God to make it clearer to our heart.

When God calls us to do something,
He also gives the faith to do it.

GOD'S WORD FOR YOU

Then Peter came up to Him and said, Lord, how many times may my brother sin against me and I forgive him and let it go? [As many as] up to seven times?

Jesus answered him, I tell you, not up to seven times, but seventy times seven!

MATTHEW 18:21–22

A FORGIVING HEART

I don't know about you, but I am glad that God does not put a limit on how many times He will forgive us. We are willing to keep taking and taking forgiveness from God, but it is amazing how little we want to give forgiveness to others. We freely accept mercy, yet it is surprising how rigid, legalistic, and merciless we can be toward others. Yet the Lord tells us plainly that if we will not forgive others, then God will not forgive us.

The bottom line is, if we are going to get along with people and have a positive attitude in life, we are going to have to do a lot of forgiving. We hurt ourselves and make ourselves miserable when we harbor bitterness, resentment, and unforgiveness toward another person. It is exactly what the devil wants to get you bound up in.

We cannot be unforgiving and have the anointing and power of God on our lives. I cannot have strife in my relationships and still have God's positive power working in me.

*God's ability helps us do things easily
that would otherwise be hard.*

GOD'S WORD FOR YOU

One of those who listened to us was a woman named Lydia, from the city of Thyatira, a dealer in fabrics dyed in purple. She was [already] a worshiper of God, and the Lord opened her heart to pay attention to what was said by Paul.

ACTS 16:14

An Open Heart

Lydia was used to living under the Jewish Law, and Paul came to the city of Philippi delivering a message of grace. The reason an open heart is so important is that it allowed her to listen to this new and different message. It is amazing the things in the Bible we will refuse to believe because they are not part of what we have been taught in the past.

God wants us to be single-minded, not narrow-minded. We must have an open heart. It will tell us when what we are hearing is true. Our mind may be closed, but our heart must be open to God to allow Him to do new things in our life—not weird, off-the-wall things, but new things. Our hearts must always be open to the truth.

How often do we approach a teaching or a person with a bias or opinion, often without even realizing it. We have prejudices that have been placed in us by others through the things they have said to us. That's why we have to carefully examine our heart to see if it is open to the truth.

People who have wisdom are always willing to learn something new.

GOD'S WORD FOR YOU

But thank God, though you were once slaves of sin, you have become obedient with all your heart to the standard of teaching in which you were instructed and to which you were committed.

ROMANS 6:17

An Obedient Heart

Paul wrote that the believers in Rome were obedient with all their heart. I have also discovered that it is possible to be obedient in behavior and not be obedient with the heart. It is not just a matter of putting on a show, but a matter of having the right attitude of heart.

I want to encourage you to come up higher in your obedience. Be quick to obey, radical in your obedience, extreme in your obedience. Don't be the kind of person God has to deal with for weeks just to get you to do the simplest little thing. Just do it!

We must be obedient to God whether we feel like it or not, and we must do it with a good attitude. Our obedience to God will ultimately always be rewarded. He is always trying to get us to sow the seed that is necessary to bring another blessing into our lives. We cannot outgive God; it is impossible.

A lifestyle of obedience to God brings rewards with it. The devil will give up when he sees you are not going to give in.

GOD'S WORD FOR YOU

Blessed are the pure in heart: for they shall see God.

MATTHEW 5:8 KJV

A PURE HEART

In Psalm 51:6, David tells us that having a pure heart means having truth in our inner being, which is the real person. It's all about paying attention to our thought life because out of it come our words, our emotions, our attitudes, and our motives.

Purity of heart is not a natural trait. It is something that must be worked on in most of us. In 1 John 3:3 we see that we should desire and work toward purity of heart because it is God's will.

There is a price to pay to have a pure heart, but there is also a reward. We don't have to be afraid to make the commitment to allow God to do a deep work in us. We may not always feel comfortable about the truths He will bring to us, but if we will take care of our part, God will take care of making sure that we are blessed.

God is an expert at removing worthless things out of us while retaining the valuable.

THE MIND
OF CHRIST

Believe what the Word says you are,
and that is what you will become.
Believe what the devil says you are,
and you will become that.
The choice is yours.

GOD'S WORD FOR YOU

For who has known or understood the mind (the counsels and purposes) of the Lord so as to guide and instruct Him and give Him knowledge? But we have the mind of Christ (the Messiah) and do hold the thoughts (feelings and purposes) of His heart.

1 CORINTHIANS 2:16

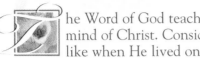

six

THE MIND OF CHRIST

he Word of God teaches us that we have the mind of Christ. Consider what His mind was like when He lived on the earth, and then consider what your mind is like. If your mind wanders all over the place, if you get upset and confused, or if your mind is full of doubt and unbelief, you are not experiencing all that God desires for your life.

Let me remind you that the renewal of the mind is a process that requires time, and it's a process that Satan aggressively fights against. We have to purposely choose right thinking. When we feel the battle for our mind is too difficult, we must determine that we are going to make it. It is vitally important that we choose life-generating thoughts.

The renewing of the mind takes place little by little, so don't be discouraged if progress seems slow. Take a stand and say, "I will never give up! God is on my side. He loves me, and He is helping me!"

Our thoughts are silent words that only we
and the Lord hear, but those words affect our inner man,
our health, our joy, and our attitudes.

GOD'S WORD FOR YOU

Do two walk together except they make an appointment and have agreed?

AMOS 3:3

THINK POSITIVE THOUGHTS

If you are thinking according to the mind of Christ, your thoughts will be positive. Enough can never be said about the power of being positive. God is positive, and if you want to flow with Him, you must get on the same wavelength and begin to think positively. I am not talking about exercising mind control, but simply about being an all-around, positive person.

Have a positive outlook and attitude. Maintain positive thoughts and expectations. Engage in positive conversation. Notice that throughout His life Jesus endured tremendous difficulties, including personal attacks, and yet He remained ever positive. He always had an uplifting comment, an encouraging word. He always gave hope to those He came near.

Allow God to be the glory and lifter of your head (Psalm 3:3). He wants to lift everything: our hopes, our attitudes, our moods, our head, hands, and heart—our life. He is our divine Lifter!

Remember, you become what you think.
Change your thinking and be set free!

GOD'S WORD FOR YOU

You will guard him and keep him in perfect and constant peace whose mind [both its inclination and its character] is stayed on You, because he commits himself to You, leans on You, and hopes confidently in You.

ISAIAH 26:3

As for me, I will continue beholding Your face in righteousness (rightness, justice, and right standing with You); I shall be fully satisfied, when I awake [to find myself] beholding Your form [and having sweet communion with You].

PSALM 17:15

I will meditate also upon all Your works and consider all Your [mighty] deeds.

PSALM 77:12

$\mathscr{B}$E GOD-MINDED

Jesus had a continual fellowship with His heavenly Father. It is impossible to have full fellowship with anyone without having your mind on that individual. The thoughts of a person functioning in the mind of Christ would be on God and on all His mighty works.

It is tremendously uplifting to think on the goodness of God and all the marvelous works of His hands. If you want to experience victory, you must make meditation a regular part of your thought life. Fellowshiping with God is the one sure way to begin enjoying life.

Jesus said that the Holy Spirit would bring us into close fellowship with Him (John 16:7). If we will fill our mind with the Lord, it will bring Him into our consciousness, and we will begin to enjoy a fellowship with Him that brings joy, peace, and victory to our everyday life.

❧

Jesus is always with us, but we need to think on Him and be aware of His presence.

GOD'S WORD FOR YOU

And we know (understand, recognize, are conscious of, by observation and by experience) and believe (adhere to and put faith in and rely on) the love God cherishes for us. God is love, and he who dwells and continues in love dwells and continues in God, and God dwells and continues in him.

1 JOHN 4:16

BE GOD-LOVES-ME-MINDED

I have learned that the same thing is true of God's love that is true of His presence. If we never meditate on His love for us, we will not experience it.

Paul prayed in Ephesians 3 that the people would experience the love of God for themselves. The Bible says that He loves us. But how many of God's children still lack a revelation concerning His love?

First John 4:16 states that we should be conscious, actively aware of God's love. The love of God is meant to be a powerful force in our lives, one that will take us through even the most difficult trials into victory.

I became conscious of God's love for me through learning Scriptures about His love. I meditated on them and confessed them out of my mouth. I did this over and over for months, and all the time the revelation of His unconditional love for me was becoming more and more of a reality for me.

Let the love of God be strong in your weaknesses. God's love is the foundation upon which Christian living must stand.

GOD'S WORD FOR YOU

There is no fear in love; but perfect love casteth out fear.

1 JOHN 4:18 KJV

For our sake He made Christ [virtually] to be sin Who knew no sin, so that in and through Him we might become [endued with, viewed as being in, and examples of] the righteousness of God [what we ought to be, approved and acceptable and in right relationship with Him, by His goodness].

2 CORINTHIANS 5:21

$\mathscr{B}$E RIGHTEOUSNESS–CONSCIOUS

Believers operating with the mind of Christ are not going to think about how terrible they are. They will have righteousness-based thoughts that come through meditating regularly on who they are "in Christ."

Yet a large number of believers are tormented by negative thoughts about how sinful they are, or how displeased God is with them because of all their weaknesses and failures. How much time is wasted living under guilt and condemnation?

Think about how you have been made the righteousness of God in Christ Jesus. Remember: Thoughts turn into actions. If you want to behave any better, you have to align your thinking with God's Word. Every time a negative, condemning thought comes to your mind, remind yourself that God loves you, and that you have been made righteous in Christ.

You are changing for the better all the time.
Every day you're growing spiritually. God has
a glorious plan for your life!

GOD'S WORD FOR YOU

He who exhorts (encourages), to his exhortation.

ROMANS 12:8

Have an Exhortative Mind

The person with the mind of Christ thinks positive, uplifting, edifying thoughts about other people as well as about himself and his own circumstances. You never exhort anyone with your words if you have not first had kind thoughts about that individual. Remember that whatever is in your heart will come out of your mouth. Thoughts and words are containers or weapons for carrying creative or destructive power. Do some "love thinking" on purpose.

Send thoughts of love toward other people. Speak words of encouragement. Come alongside others and urge them to press forward in their spiritual life. Bring words that make others feel better and that encourage them to press on.

Everyone has enough problems already. We don't need to add to their troubles by tearing them down. We should build up one another in love (Ephesians 4:29). Love always believes the best of everyone (1 Corinthians 13:7).

We are not walking in the Word if our thoughts and words are opposite of what it says.

GOD'S WORD FOR YOU

Enter into His gates with thanksgiving and a thank offering and into His courts with praise! Be thankful and say so to Him, bless and affectionately praise His name!

PSALM 100:4

Through Him, therefore, let us constantly and at all times offer up to God a sacrifice of praise, which is the fruit of lips that thankfully acknowledge and confess and glorify His name.

HEBREWS 13:15

DEVELOP A THANKFUL MIND

A person flowing in the mind of Christ will find his thoughts filled with praise and thanksgiving. A powerful life cannot be lived without thanksgiving. The Bible instructs us over and over in the principle of thanksgiving. It is a life principle.

Many doors are opened to the enemy through complaining. Some people are physically ill and live weak, powerless lives due to this disease called complaining that attacks the thoughts and conversations of people.

We are to offer thanksgiving at all times—in every situation, in all things—and by so doing enter into the victorious life where the devil cannot control us. It may require a sacrifice of praise or thanksgiving, but be a grateful person—one filled with gratitude not only toward God but also toward people. Expressing appreciation is not only good for the other person, but it is good for us, because it releases joy in us.

God delights in giving His children favor.
Offer thanksgiving to God, and as you do
you will find your heart filling with life and light.

GOD'S WORD FOR YOU

And you have not His word (His thought) living in your hearts, because you do not believe and adhere to and trust in and rely on Him Whom He has sent. [That is why you do not keep His message living in you, because you do not believe in the Messenger Whom He has sent.]

JOHN 5:38

BE WORD-MINDED

God's Word is His thoughts written down on paper for our study and consideration. His Word is how He thinks about every situation and subject. Anyone who wants to experience all the good results of believing must allow His Word to be a living message in their heart. This is accomplished by meditating on the Word of God. This is how His thoughts become our thoughts—the only way to develop the mind of Christ in us.

Joshua 1:8 tells us plainly that we will never put the Word into practice physically if we don't first practice it mentally. Meditating on (attending to, pondering, thinking about) the Word of God even has the power to affect our physical body. Proverbs 4:20–22 tells us that the words of the Lord are a source of health and healing to the flesh.

Remember the principle of sowing and reaping. The greater the amount of time you and I personally put into thinking about and studying the Word, the more we will get out of it. The Lord reveals His secrets to those who are diligent about the Word.

Words are seeds. What we speak we sow, and what we sow, we reap!

GOD'S WORD FOR YOU

Now the mind of the flesh [which is sense and reason without the Holy Spirit] is death [death that comprises all the miseries arising from sin, both here and hereafter]. But the mind of the [Holy] Spirit is life and [soul] peace [both now and forever].

ROMANS 8:6

For the rest, brethren, whatever is true, whatever is worthy of reverence and is honorable and seemly, whatever is just, whatever is pure, whatever is lovely and lovable, whatever is kind and winsome and gracious, if there is any virtue and excellence, if there is anything worthy of praise, think on and weigh and take account of these things [fix your minds on them].

PHILIPPIANS 4:8

Always Choose Life!

The condition of your mind should be as described by Paul in Philippians 4:8. You have the mind of Christ, so begin to use it. If He wouldn't think it, you shouldn't think it either.

Think about what you are thinking about. Satan usually deceives people into thinking that the source of their misery or trouble is something other than what it really is. It is by this continual "watching over" your thoughts that you begin to take every thought captive unto the obedience of Jesus Christ (2 Corinthians 10:5).

The Holy Spirit is quick to remind you if your mind is beginning to take you in a negative direction. If you continue, then the decision becomes yours. Will you flow in the mind of the flesh or in the mind of the Spirit? One leads to death, the other to life. The choice is yours.

Choose life!

*A person will get out of the Word
what he is willing to put into it.*

JOYCE MEYER

Joyce Meyer has been teaching the Word of God since 1976 and in full-time ministry since 1980. She is the bestselling author of over 54 inspirational books, including *Secrets to Exceptional Living*, *The Joy of Believing Prayer*, and *Battlefield of the Mind*, as well as over 240 audiocassette albums and over 90 videos. Joyce's *Life In The Word* radio and television programs are broadcast around the world, and she travels extensively conducting "Life In The Word" conferences. Joyce and her husband, Dave, are the parents of four grown children and make their home in St. Louis, Missouri.

Additional copies of this book are available from your local bookstore.

If this book has changed your life, we would like to hear from you.

Please write us at:

Joyce Meyer Ministries
P.O. Box 655 • Fenton, MO 63026

or call: (636) 349-0303

Internet Address: www.joycemeyer.org

In Canada, write: Joyce Meyer Ministries Canada, Inc.
Lambeth Box 1300 • London, ON N6P 1T5

or call: (636) 349-0303

In Australia, write: Joyce Meyer Ministries—Australia
Locked Bag 77 • Mansfield Delivery Centre
Queensland 4122

or call: (07) 3349 1200

In England, write: Joyce Meyer Ministries
P.O. Box 1549 • Windsor • SL4 1GT

or call: 01753 831102